GALLBLADDER

lub-DUB
lub-DUB

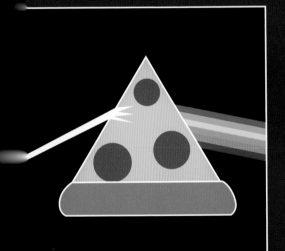

BRAIN

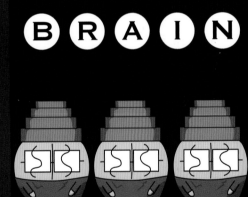

Fat

BOWELS

Lungs

B R A I N WAVES

Special thanks to Adam M. Robin, neurosurgical oncologist at Henry Ford Health System, for his guidance and expert modification of the information included in this book.

For Calan, Emmett, and Nola — you're all a Big Deal.

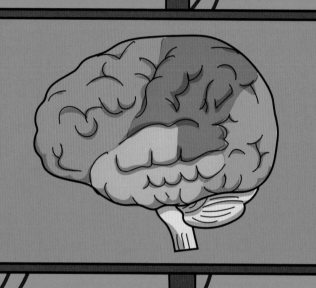

First edition, October 2019
Book design by Kirk Benshoff
Copyright © 2019 by Nick Seluk

10 9 8 7 6 5 4 3 2 1
19 20 21 22 23

ISBN: 978-1-338-16700-9

Library of Congress
Cataloging-in-Publication Data
available

From the NEW YORK TIMES bestselling creator of HEART AND BRAIN

THE BRAIN IS KIND OF A BIG DEAL

Solo Artist
of the Year

Nick Seluk

Orchard Books • New York • An Imprint of Scholastic Inc.

Inside of your head, behind your eyes, and under your hair is one of the coolest things about you: your **BRAIN**.

Your brain is the command center of your entire body. A living computer! It's constantly collecting and storing new information about everything you **experience**. That way, the next time you experience the same thing, your brain will know exactly what to do!

Heart

Lungs

Muscles

Stomach

Ears

Tongue

Eyes

Nose

Inte

Without your brain, you wouldn't be able to read
and understand these words, or even turn the page!

Sure—for you, turning the page seemed easy! But your brain had to move a lot of different muscles in just the right way to make that happen. Your brain works really hard all the time without you even knowing it.

Great work, Muscle.

I just needed to flex a bit.

You can do it!

SMART STUFF

Scientists have been learning about the brain for a very long time, but they still don't know everything! It's so complex we may never learn all there is to know, but scientists will never stop trying to discover more!

Within your brain are five sections called **lobes**. Each lobe does something a little different, but the parts all work together, too.

The brain is made up of billions of things called **neurons**. They talk to one another by sending messages through gaps called **synapses**. When your brain's neurons work together to help your body take action, you can do all kinds of complicated things.

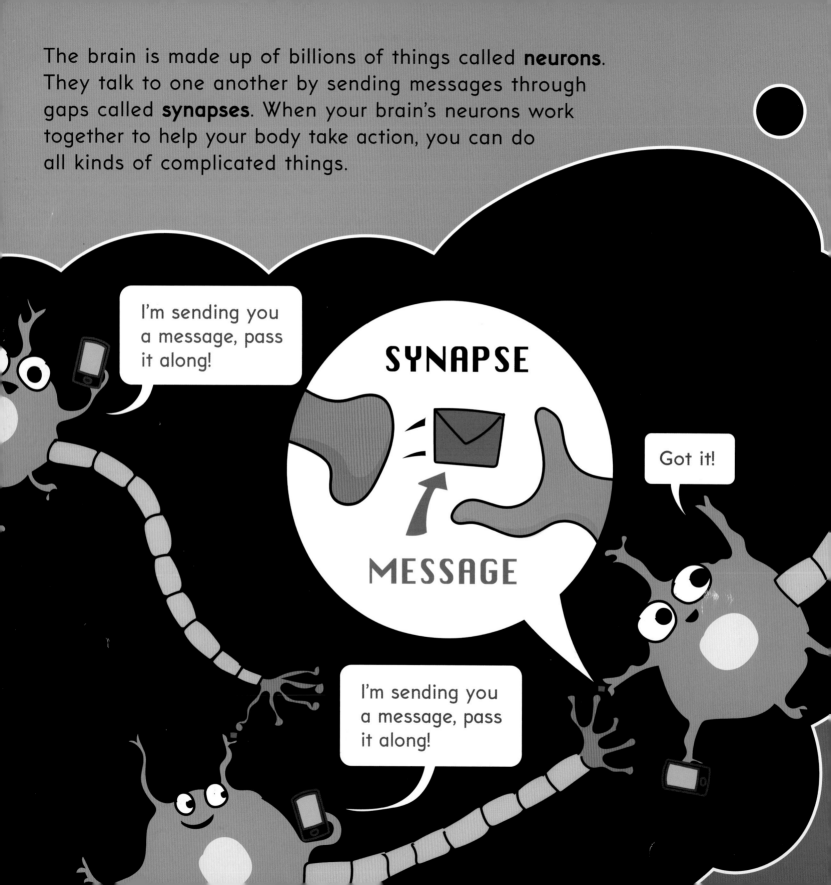

Your brain also uses nerves to get messages back from the rest of your body. If you get a paper cut or scrape your knee, a nerve will let your brain know very quickly!

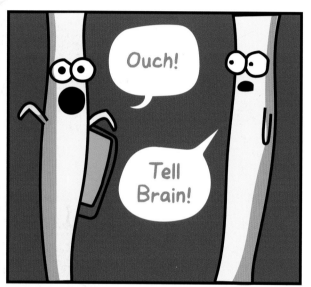

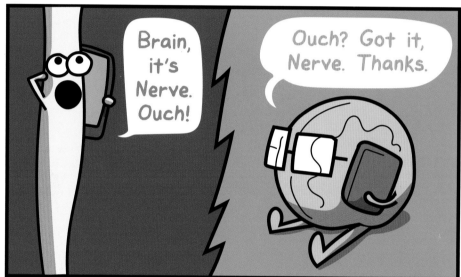

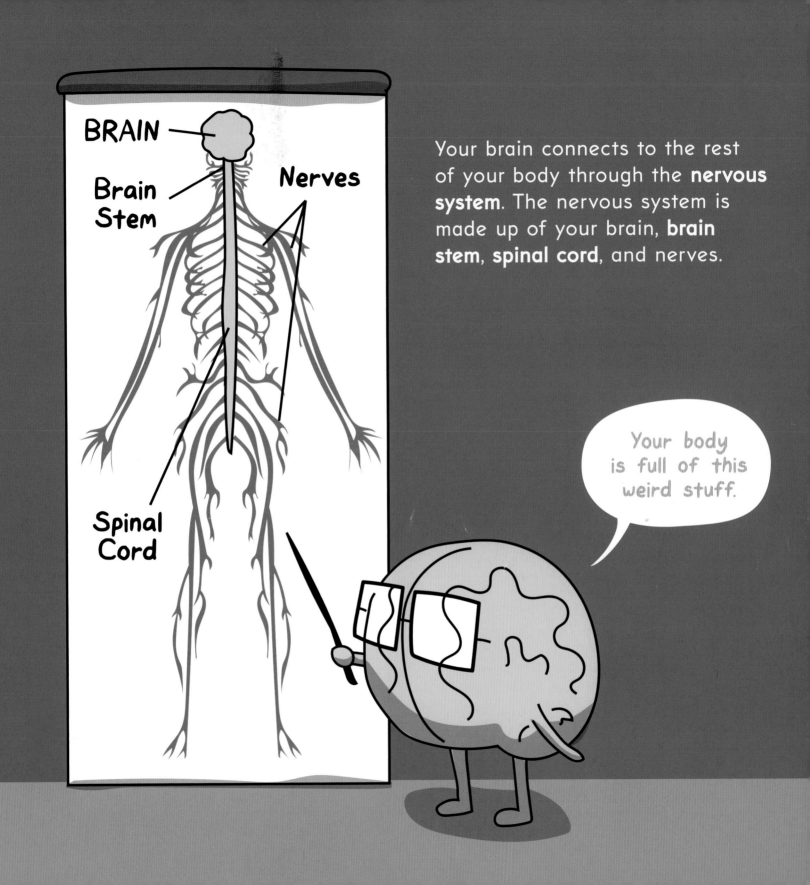

Your brain connects to the rest of your body through the **nervous system**. The nervous system is made up of your brain, **brain stem**, **spinal cord**, and nerves.

Your brain makes your body do a lot of important things that keep you alive without you even thinking about it, like telling your heart to beat and . . .

your lungs to breathe.

INVOLUNTARY vs. VOLUNTARY

When your brain does something for your body that you don't have to think about, it's called an **involuntary function**.

Examples of Involuntary Functions

Tear production
Blinking
Sweating
Digesting food in your stomach!

You can choose to make your brain do stuff, too. When you do something because you want to, that's a **voluntary function**.

Examples of Voluntary Functions

Talking
Walking
Reading
Cleaning your room!

Your brain tells you when you need to eat. Your stomach and gut send messages to your brain, and your brain decides when you're hungry or full.

Are you tired right now? If you are, your brain is getting messages from your body that you need to sleep soon. When you sleep, your brain and body get a lot of much-needed rest. While you dream, your brain gets ready for the next day.

Sometimes it dreams about weird stuff.

Now it's time to move on to even more fun stuff!
The stuff that makes you YOU.

Your brain helps you turn thoughts into words so you can say or write what you're thinking. When you talk and write in a way that other people understand, you're using **language**.

BRAIN (ENGLISH)
CEREBRO (SPANISH)
腦 (CHINESE)

Now I can talk about myself all over the world!

SMART STUFF

People speak different languages all over the world! Depending on where you grow up, you might speak a different language with different words. Many people even speak more than one language, which allows them to talk to even more people!

Remember how the brain collects information like a computer and keeps it for later? Your brain is really good at using this information to figure stuff out, along with the senses:

SIGHT: Green and Brown
SOUND: Rustling
TOUCH: Rough
TASTE: Gross

RESULT: TREE!

When you see something, a message is passed from the back of your eyes to the very back of your brain.

When the brain gets the message, the images are actually upside down and backward. Your brain is a good problem solver, though!

Your ears are always listening.

It sounds kind of buzzy!

Don't tell me... Don't tell me...

It's a fly!

When you hear something, whether it's the ocean or a song or a burp, your brain has to work to understand it. The sounds that you hear are made into messages that are sent to your brain. Then your brain tells you what the sound is.

Anytime you feel with your sense of touch, like something soft or wet, messages are sent to your brain. When you touch something, your brain's experience can be really useful, especially if whatever you've touched is sharp or too hot. Then your brain can help you avoid it to keep you safe.

When a smell enters your nose, a message is sent to your brain. Your brain will then know if the smell is good or bad, or if you have smelled it before.

LATER...

Your brain is especially good at remembering smells.

When you taste something, your brain gets messages about the different flavors from your tongue. Then your brain decides if it likes the taste or not.

Your sense of taste has a lot to do with your sense of smell. Your brain uses your nose even more than your tongue to decide if something tastes good!

Your brain is also in charge of telling your muscles and body exactly how to move. When you run, your brain gives your body very specific instructions.

When you are in danger, your brain is firing messages all throughout your nervous system to make movements happen.

By now, you know that your brain is always collecting information like a computer.

All that information is stored in your **memory**. Your brain searches through all that information so you can find a memory when you need it.

A new memory is kept by your brain for about 30 seconds before it is forgotten. This is called **short-term memory**.

If you repeat something enough times, or if it's really important, that short-term memory could turn into **long-term memory**.

Long-term memories last, you guessed it, a LONG time. Don't worry, your brain will NEVER stop making new memories, so keep learning!

Something the brain is really, really good at is thinking. Thinking and thinking and thinking. Your brain is thinking about things pretty much all the time.

To think or not to think? I think I'll think.

You can imagine things and solve problems just by thinking about them. Every invention that people ever created, from rockets and medicine to toilets and pizza, came from thinking about ways to make things better!

Did you know your feelings, like love, come from your brain, too?

You feel happy, sad, angry, or scared without ever having to learn how. You can control how you react when you feel something, but your feelings happen no matter what.

Your brain is pretty important.

It helps you makes sense of the world around you. It tells your heart to pump blood to the rest of your body and your lungs to breathe so you can stay alive. It moves your body and helps you talk, see, and hear.

Your brain is in charge of all the thoughts, feelings, and memories that make you YOU.

That's kind of a big deal.

GLOSSARY

BRAIN: THE ORGAN INSIDE YOUR CRANIUM THAT CONTROLS YOUR BODY'S ACTIVITIES, THOUGHTS, MEMORIES, AND EMOTIONS

BRAIN STEM: THE PART OF YOUR BRAIN THAT CONNECTS TO YOUR SPINAL CORD AND CONTAINS THE CENTERS THAT CONTROL INVOLUNTARY FUNCTIONS LIKE BREATHING

EXPERIENCE: SOMETHING THAT HAPPENS TO YOU

FRONTAL LOBE: THE FRONT PORTION OF YOUR BRAIN RESPONSIBLE FOR MOTIVATION, DECISION-MAKING, LANGUAGE EXPRESSION, AND PARTS OF YOUR PERSONALITY

INSULAR LOBE: A SECTION DEEP INSIDE THE BRAIN THAT HELPS YOU UNDERSTAND WHAT YOUR BODY EXPERIENCES AND MAY HOUSE SPEECH AND MOTOR FUNCTIONS

INVOLUNTARY FUNCTION: SOMETHING THAT IS DONE WITHOUT A PERSON'S CONTROL

LANGUAGE: THE USE OF WORDS TO COMMUNICATE THOUGHTS AND FEELINGS

LOBE: ONE SECTION OF A BODY PART OR ORGAN

LONG-TERM MEMORY: SOMETHING YOU CAN REMEMBER OVER A LONG PERIOD OF TIME

MEMORY: A THOUGHT OF SOMETHING THAT YOU REMEMBER FROM THE PAST

NERVES: THE THREADS THAT SEND MESSAGES BETWEEN YOUR BRAIN AND SPINAL CORD TO OTHER PARTS OF YOUR BODY SO YOU CAN MOVE AND FEEL

NERVOUS SYSTEM: A SYSTEM IN THE BODY THAT INCLUDES THE BRAIN, SPINAL CORD, AND NERVES. IN HUMANS AND ANIMALS, THE NERVOUS SYSTEM CONTROLS ALL THE FEELINGS AND ACTIONS OF THE BODY.

NEURONS: THE CELLS THAT CARRY INFORMATION BETWEEN THE BRAIN AND OTHER PARTS OF THE BODY

OCCIPITAL LOBE: THE BACK PORTION OF YOUR BRAIN THAT HELPS YOU UNDERSTAND WHAT YOU SEE

PARIETAL LOBE: THE SECTION OF YOUR BRAIN BETWEEN THE FRONTAL AND OCCIPITAL LOBES THAT DEALS WITH SENSATIONS LIKE TOUCH AND PAIN AND BEING AWARE

SHORT-TERM MEMORY: SOMETHING YOU CAN ONLY REMEMBER FOR A SHORT PERIOD OF TIME

SPINAL CORD: A THICK CORD OF NERVE TISSUE THAT STARTS BELOW THE BRAIN AND BRAIN STEM AND RUNS THROUGH THE SPINAL CANAL WITHIN THE SPINAL COLUMN

SYNAPSE: THE LOCATION WHERE TWO NEURONS COMMUNICATE AND PASS MESSAGES

TEMPORAL LOBE: THE BOTTOM SECTION OF YOUR BRAIN THAT IS MAINLY IN CHARGE OF YOUR HEARING AND MEMORY

VOLUNTARY FUNCTION: SOMETHING THAT IS DONE ON PURPOSE FOR A SPECIFIC REASON

WILD FACTS ABOUT ANIMAL BRAINS

Dolphins have larger brains than humans. Their brains are also very complex, especially in the sections that deal with problem-solving, emotions, and self-awareness. This means they are some of the smartest animals on Earth (besides humans).

EE EE EEEE EE!!!

Some of the biggest dinosaurs—like *Stegosaurus*—had very small brains compared to their body size. These giant dinosaurs could have had brains as small as walnuts!

Leeches' bodies are broken up into 32 internal segments. Each segment has its own mini brain!

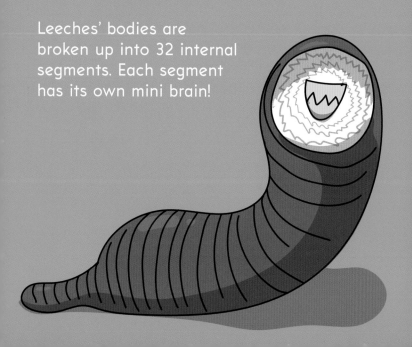

Each of an ostrich's huge eyes is bigger than its brain! That means its brain is pretty small. No wonder they run in circles to avoid predators.

Sea squirts eat their own brains! When a sea squirt is done developing, it settles into the sea floor where it stays for the rest of its life. Then it absorbs its little brain since it doesn't need it to move around anymore.

I'm tired of moving.

Okay, let's stop. Time for dinner!

A cockroach can live for weeks without its head and brain. And the antennae on its head can still move back and forth for hours after it's removed from its body!

Are you okay?

Why wouldn't I be okay?

Sea stars don't have brains. Instead, they have nerves that help them with basic things, like finding food.

I don't think, therefore... I'm...not?

A woodpecker has air pockets in its head. This is extra protection that keeps its brain safe from injuries while they are pecking at trees.

What was I doing? Oh right! I was banging my beak on a tree.

Brain

Command center of the body.
Lead vocals.

100 Billion
Followers

Recent Posts

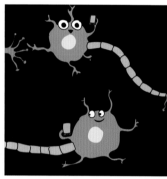

Tongue
Elite Food Snob

10,048 Reviews

Most recent reviews

Pizza ★★★★★
"Pizza iss alwaysss ssoo good."

Not Pizza ★
"WHO INVENTED THISSS?"

Stomach
Health
Blogger

Recent blog posts:

Probiotics and you!
Bacteria can be good! Here's how probiotics are good for your gut.

Too much of a good thing
Does Tongue really have your best interests in mind?